■SCHOLASTIC

GREAT STATES
Quilt Math

by Cindi Mitchell

NEW YORK • TORONTO • LONDON • AUCKLAND • SYDNEY
MEXICO CITY • NEW DELHI • HONG KONG • BUENOS AIRES

Teaching
Resources

This book is dedicated to my daughter, Jeannine Mitchell.
Just like a patchwork quilt, she is warm and cozy, sweet and dainty
all quilted together with little stitches of irresistible love!

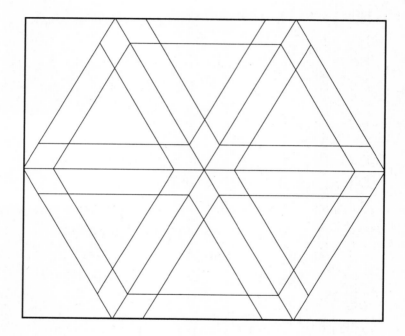

Cover and interior design by Brian LaRossa
Illustrations by Cindi, Ben, and Jim Mitchell

ISBN: 0-439-42067-9
Copyright © 2006 by Cindi Mitchell
Published by Scholastic Inc.
All rights reserved.
Printed in U.S.A.

1 2 3 4 5 6 7 8 9 10   40   13 12 11 10 09 08 07 06 05

Contents

Continued

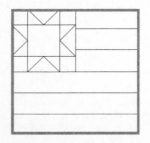
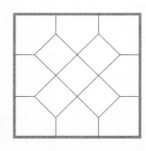
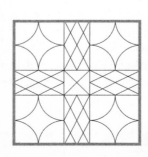
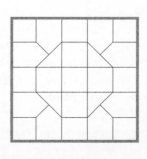

Introduction

A student of mine once asked me how she could improve her daily math grades and raise her test scores. I told her that math is like everything else in life: to improve your skills you need to practice, practice, practice!

The interactive pages in this book will give your students repeated practice of essential math skills to help them build mastery and automaticity, and help them do better on tests. At the same time, they will learn interesting facts about each of the 50 states and have fun coloring quilt blocks from each state. Here's how it works:

There are 50 quilt blocks in this book—one for each state. Each quilt block contains math problems for students to solve. After completing all of the math problems, students color their quilt block using the key near the bottom of the page as a guide. Reading the key gives students practice in following directions and additional practice in math. Students will need a 16-pack of crayons or colored pencils to color their quilt blocks.

In the boxes to the left of the quilt block on each page, students will learn information about the state, including the official state tree, flower, bird, and capital. An outline of the state and a picture of its flag also appears. Finally, a State Challenge word problem reinforces the math skill on the page and includes other facts about the state. (An answer key for these questions begins on page 60 followed by Suggested Resources.)

To help you connect the activities in this book with your curriculum, the Contents on pages 3–4 organizes the activities by state name, skill area, and page number. You can see at a glance the activities that match the math skill you are teaching. The skill focus of each activity also appears in the upper right corner of each activity page.

The last three activities in the book (pages 57-59) give students the opportunity to create quilt block designs about their own state. Challenge students further by trying some of the Taking It Further activities on the next page.

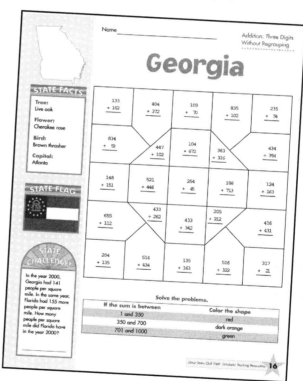

About the State Quilt Blocks

Since there are no official quilt blocks for each state, you might wonder how I chose the quilt blocks to include in this book. In the early 1900s, a magazine called *Hearth & Home* asked readers from around the country to send quilt blocks that they felt represented their state. The editors at *Hearth & Home* chose what they considered the best quilt block from each state and published them in their magazine. (Later, the magazine published designs for what were then the territories of Alaska and Hawaii, which are also included here.) Whenever possible, I used the state quilt blocks published in *Hearth & Home*. Some adaptations have been made for simplicity.

Taking It Further

★ Design a State Quilt Block

Invite students to create an original quilt block design on grid paper that represents their state. Encourage them to use the design to make a quilt block by simply cutting shapes from colored construction paper and gluing them onto a background sheet of paper.

★ Fun With Color

Give students the opportunity to color their state quilt block with colors of their choice. First, find the activity page for your state. Mask the color words listed in the key and make a copy of the page for each student. Invite students to write in colors of their choice and then color the quilt box accordingly. You might want to display the pictures and discuss the effects of color selection on quilt design.

★ Quilt Block Shapes

Encourage students to look at the different quilt designs in the book and identify the different shapes they see. Point out that some quilt blocks are made with only one or two geometric shapes. For instance, the Alabama quilt block (page 7), includes only squares and rectangles and the Connecticut quilt block (page 13), is composed of different sizes and types of triangles. Challenge students to create their own quilt block using only one or two geometric shapes. Tell them that they can vary the size of the shapes if they wish. (For additional resources about quilts, see page 63.)

★ Favorite State Notecard

Cut white construction paper into 6- by 12-inch inch pieces. Give one piece to each student. Tell students to fold the paper in half the short way to make a 6- by 6-inch square notecard. Ask each student to identify his or her favorite state. It might be the state where they were born, a state they would like to visit, or one that has a unique manmade or natural landmark. Invite students to design and color a quilt block square on the front of the notecard that depicts the state of their choice. Inside, ask students to write the name of their state and explain why they chose it.

★ Math Imagination

Invite students to create a quilt block activity page like the ones in this book. Have them design a quilt block and place math problems inside the shapes. At the bottom of the page they should include a key for coloring. Encourage children to trade activity pages with their classmates to complete.

★ State Data Tally

As students read the facts provided for each state, they may notice that several states are represented by the same symbols. For example, the Cardinal is the official state bird for seven different states, while the Mockingbird and the Meadowlark each represent six different states. Encourage students to look for states that have the same official bird, flower, or tree, and tally and report on the data they collect.

Alabama

STATE FACTS

Tree:
Southern pine

Flower:
Camellia

Bird:
Yellowhammer

Capital:
Montgomery

STATE FLAG

STATE CHALLENGE!

On December 14, 1819, Alabama was the 22nd state to be admitted into the Union. Record the number of tens and ones in the number 22.

tens _____

ones _____

40	18								57
	69	99					58		
22	88	55	10			47	75	27	
		11	44	71	50	22			
			72	34	93				
			43	82	67				
	62	31				62			
41	70						53		
46	19								56

Look at the digits in the tens place.

If the digit is	Color the shape
1, 2, or 3	orange
4, 5, or 6	yellow
7, 8, or 9	green

Name _____

Alaska

STATE FACTS

Tree:
Sitka spruce

Flower:
Forget-me-not

Bird:
Willow ptarmigan

Capital:
Juneau

STATE FLAG

STATE CHALLENGE!

The highest point in Alaska is Mount McKinley. It is 20,320 feet above sea level. On the line below, write the digit that is in the hundreds place in the number 20,320.

_____

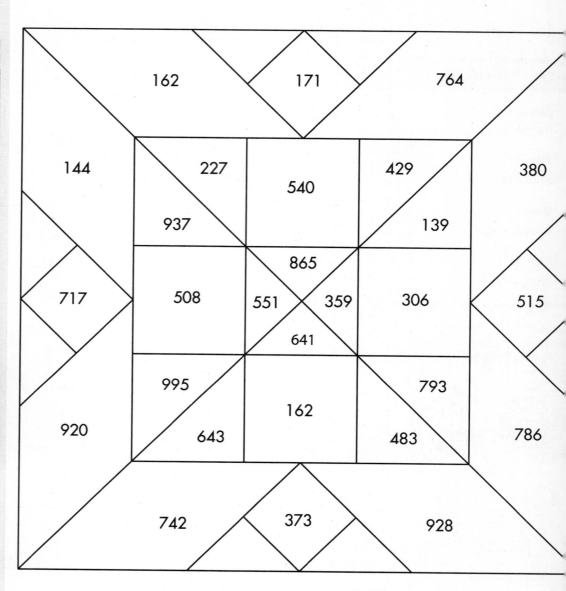

Look at each number.

If the digit in the	Color the shape
hundreds place is even	purple
tens place is odd	red
ones place is even	blue

Fill in the other shapes with colors of your choice.

Name _____

Arizona

STATE FACTS

Tree:
Paloverde

Flower:
Saguaro cactus

Bird:
Cactus wren

Capital:
Phoenix

STATE FLAG

STATE CHALLENGE!

Arizona is the home of the Grand Canyon—a beautiful canyon that was carved by the Colorado River. At its deepest point the canyon is six thousand feet. Write the number *six thousand* in standard form.

1,310	3,712	5,134	1,992
2,256	9,435	7,619	4,698
3,112	1,244	9,886	7,138
5,699	3,530	2,410	3,233
9,071	4,672	7,198	5,817
7,170	3,224	5,066	7,398
6,892	5,417	9,039	8,678
7,330	3,512	1,754	9,998

Look at each number.

If the digit in the	Color the shape
thousands place is even	yellow
hundreds place is odd	green
tens place is even	brown
ones place is odd	orange

Fill in the other shapes with colors of your choice.

Name _____

STATE FLAG

STATE CHALLENGE!

In 2004, Arkansas had an estimated population of 2,752,629. Did Arkansas have more or less than two million people in that year?

_____

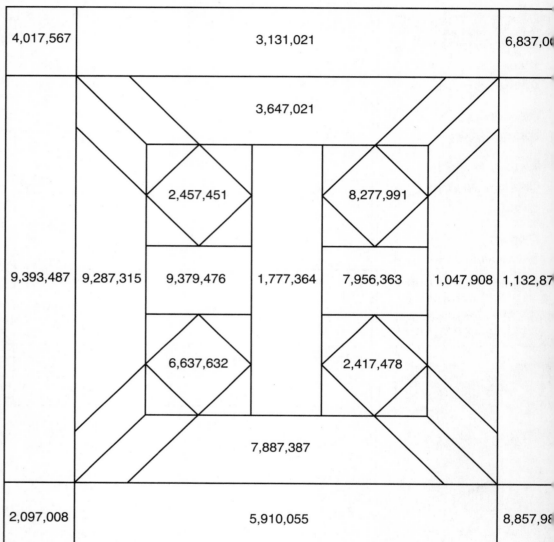

| 4,017,567 | 3,131,021 | 6,837,00 |

3,647,021

2,457,451   8,277,991

| 9,393,487 | 9,287,315 | 9,379,476 | 1,777,364 | 7,956,363 | 1,047,908 | 1,132,87 |

6,637,632   2,417,478

7,887,387

| 2,097,008 | 5,910,055 | 8,857,98 |

Look at each number.

If the digit in the	Color the shape
millions place is even	red
hundred thousands place is odd	blue
ten thousands place is even	yellow

Fill in the other shapes with colors of your choice.

Name _____

California

677,113,980,300	2,250,564,698	99,927,218,288
	8,917,197,065	84,989,075,519
700,312,286,250	8,366,134,647	566,178,578,912
	22,131,229,854	300,183,161,577
11,801,170,142	74,124,922,876	1,905,652,065

Look at each number.

If the digit in the	Color the shape
billions place is odd	purple
millions place is even	green
thousands place is odd	yellow

Colorado

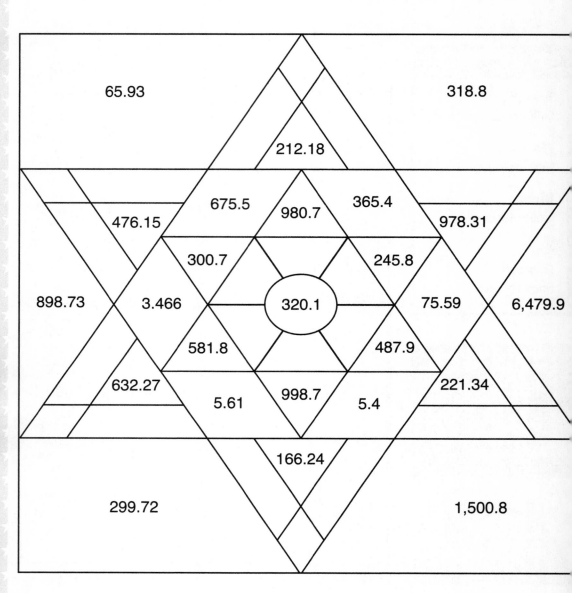

Look at the digit in the tenths place.

If the digit is	Color the shape
1, 2, or 3	yellow
4, 5, or 6	orange
7, 8, or 9	purple

Fill in the other shapes with colors of your choice.

Name _____

Connecticut

STATE CHALLENGE!

For the month of January, Connecticut's average temperature is 25.96° F. Write the word name for the decimal 25.96.

_____

_____

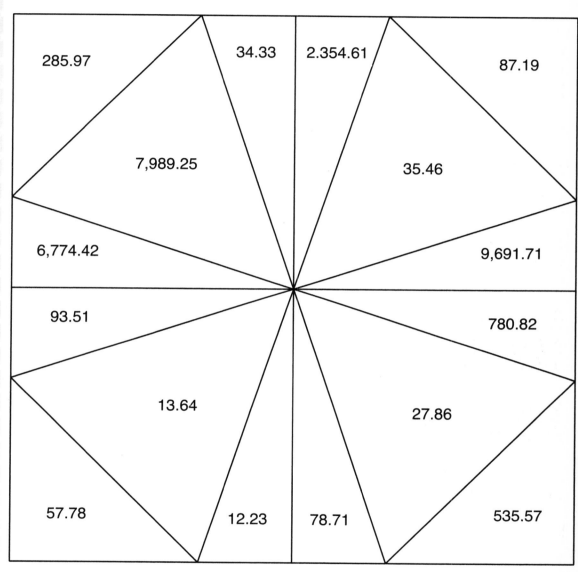

285.97 34.33 2.354.61 87.19

7,989.25 35.46

6,774.42 9,691.71

93.51 780.82

13.64 27.86

57.78 12.23 78.71 535.57

Look at the digit in the hundredths place.

If the digit is	Color the shape
1, 2, or 3	pink
4, 5, or 6	purple
7, 8, or 9	yellow

Delaware

STATE FACTS

Tree:
American holly

Flower:
Peach blossom

Bird:
Blue hen chicken

Capital:
Dover

STATE FLAG

DECEMBER 7, 1787

STATE CHALLENGE!

Delaware has 41 members in the State House of Representatives and 21 members in the State Senate. Delaware's lawmaking body has how many members in all?

_____

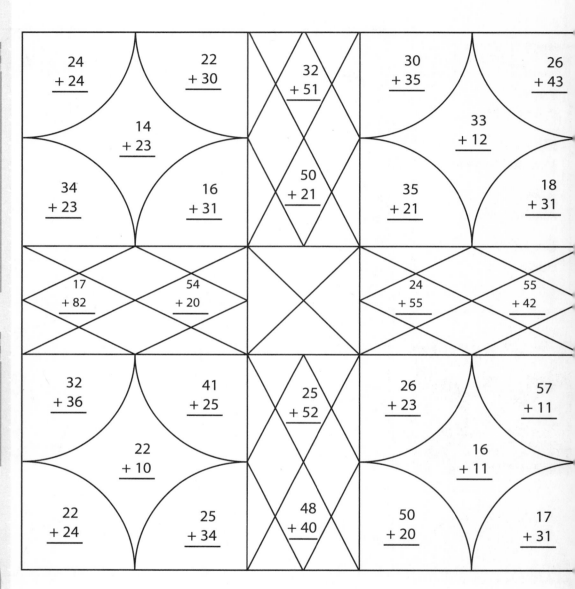

24 + 24	22 + 30	32 + 51	30 + 35	26 + 43
14 + 23			33 + 12	
34 + 23	16 + 31	50 + 21	35 + 21	18 + 31
17 + 82	54 + 20		24 + 55	55 + 42
32 + 36	41 + 25	25 + 52	26 + 23	57 + 11
22 + 10			16 + 11	
22 + 24	25 + 34	48 + 40	50 + 20	17 + 31

Solve the problems.

If the sum is between	Color the shape
1 and 45	dark blue
46 and 70	yellow
71 and 100	blue

Fill in the other shapes with colors of your choice.

Name _____

Florida

STATE FACTS

Tree:
Sabal palm

Flower:
Orange blossom

Bird:
Mockingbird

Capital:
Tallahassee

STATE FLAG

STATE CHALLENGE!

On Saturday, Shawna and Joe rode their bikes 19 miles on Florida's Van Fleet Trail and then 24 miles on the Pinellas Trail on Sunday. How many miles did they ride in all?

_____

$37 + 26 =$ _____

$\begin{array}{r} 12 \\ + 38 \\ \hline \end{array}$

$\begin{array}{r} 15 \\ + 57 \\ \hline \end{array}$

$\begin{array}{r} 19 \\ + 18 \\ \hline \end{array}$

$\begin{array}{r} 44 \\ + 38 \\ \hline \end{array}$

$\begin{array}{r} 38 \\ + 38 \\ \hline \end{array}$

$15 + 36 =$ _____

$33 + 28 =$ _____

$46 + 16 =$ _____

$24 + 29 =$ _____

$\begin{array}{r} 57 \\ + 26 \\ \hline \end{array}$

$\begin{array}{r} 65 \\ + 28 \\ \hline \end{array}$

$\begin{array}{r} 52 \\ + 39 \\ \hline \end{array}$

$\begin{array}{r} 24 \\ + 16 \\ \hline \end{array}$

$\begin{array}{r} 26 \\ + 18 \\ \hline \end{array}$

$38 + 18 =$ _____

Solve the problems.

If the sum is between	Color the shape
1 and 50	dark orange
51 and 70	orange
71 and 100	yellow

Fill in the other shapes with colors of your choice.

Name _____

Georgia

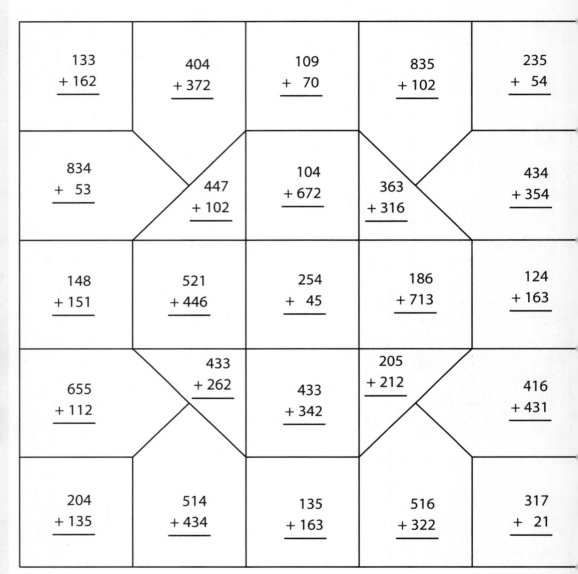

133 + 162	404 + 372	109 + 70	835 + 102	235 + 54
834 + 53	447 + 102	104 + 672	363 + 316	434 + 354
148 + 151	521 + 446	254 + 45	186 + 713	124 + 163
655 + 112	433 + 262	433 + 342	205 + 212	416 + 431
204 + 135	514 + 434	135 + 163	516 + 322	317 + 21

Solve the problems.

If the sum is between	Color the shape
1 and 350	red
350 and 700	dark orange
701 and 1000	green

Name _____

Hawaii

STATE FACTS

Tree:
Kukui (candlenut)

Flower:
Yellow hibiscus

Bird:
Nene
(Hawaiian goose)

Capital:
Honolulu

STATE FLAG

STATE CHALLENGE!

Hawaii is known for its exotic flowers. Thomas is buying boxes of Hawaiian flowers to decorate for a party. Three boxes of Hibiscus cost $134 and two boxes of Bird of Paradise cost $187. How much will all of the flowers cost?

_____

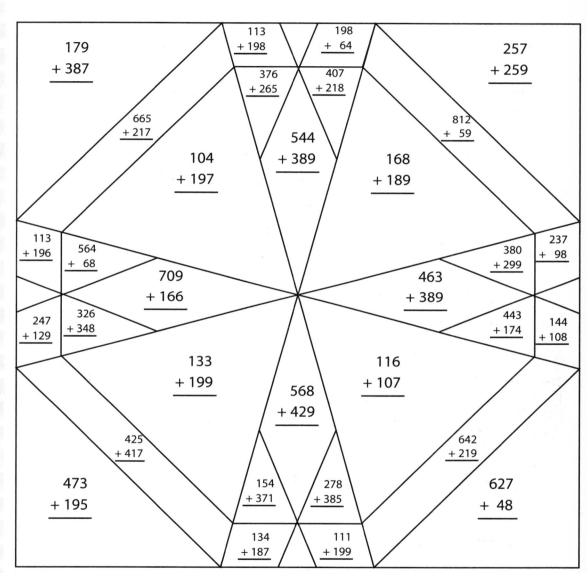

179
+ 387

113
+ 198

198
+ 64

257
+ 259

376
+ 265

407
+ 218

665
+ 217

544
+ 389

812
+ 59

104
+ 197

168
+ 189

113
+ 196

564
+ 68

380
+ 299

237
+ 98

709
+ 166

463
+ 389

247
+ 129

326
+ 348

443
+ 174

144
+ 108

133
+ 199

116
+ 107

568
+ 429

425
+ 417

642
+ 219

473
+ 195

154
+ 371

278
+ 385

627
+ 48

134
+ 187

111
+ 199

Solve the problems.

If the sum is between	Color the shape
1 and 400	orange
401 and 700	purple
701 and 1000	yellow

Fill in the other shapes with colors of your choice.

Name _____

Idaho

STATE FACTS

Tree:
Western white pine

Flower:
Syringa

Bird:
Mountain bluebird

Capital:
Boise

STATE FLAG

STATE CHALLENGE!

In the year 2000, Idaho had a population per square mile of 16. In Alabama there were 88 people per square mile. How many more people per square mile were in Alabama than Idaho?

_____

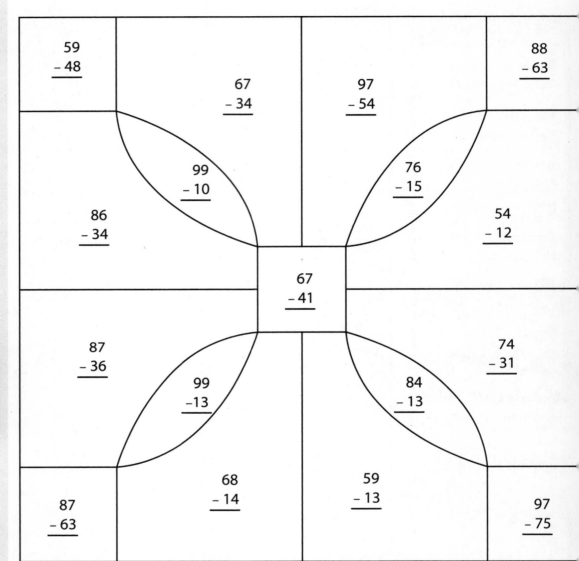

```
 59        67        97        88
-48       -34       -54       -63

      99              76
     -10             -15

 86                             54
-34                            -12

              67
             -41

 87                             74
-36                            -31

      99              84
     -13             -13

 87        68        59        97
-63       -14       -13       -75
```

**Solve the problems. Then on each line below,
write the name of a color that you like.**

If the difference is between	Color the shape
1 and 30	_____
31 and 60	_____
61 and 100	_____

Name _____

Illinois

STATE FACTS

Tree:
White oak

Flower:
Native violet

Bird:
Cardinal

Capital:
Springfield

STATE FLAG

ILLINOIS

STATE CHALLENGE!

On November 21, 1789 North Carolina was the 12th state to enter the Union. On December 3, 1818 Illinois was the 21st state to enter the Union. How many states joined the Union between these years?

_____

Quilt problems		
58 − 19	36 − 29	94 − 18
	24 − 19	74 − 28
92 − 35	87 − 69	88 − 9
	44 − 25	91 − 25
73 − 55	83 − 64	56 − 18
97 − 19	85 − 9	96 − 89
73 − 36	53 − 39	71 − 55
93 − 16	95 − 8	
50 − 48	42 − 29	93 − 55
54 − 27	52 − 38	93 − 78
68 − 9	96 − 18	83 − 25
40 − 38	56 − 39	
73 − 27	83 − 7	95 − 48
43 − 34	95 − 77	

Solve the problems.

If the difference is between	Color the shape
1 and 20	yellow
21 and 50	brown
51 and 70	orange
71 and 100	red

Name _____

Indiana

STATE FACTS

Tree:
Tulip tree

Flower:
Peony

Bird:
Cardinal

Capital:
Indianapolis

STATE FLAG

STATE CHALLENGE!

Indiana is about 270 miles long. Its width is about 130 miles less than its length. About how wide is the state of Indiana?

_____

692 − 302	986 − 305
	758 − 523
868 − 131	766 − 334
899 − 261	837 − 331
908 − 201	
654 − 402	575 − 241
476 − 235	867 − 461
536 − 421	
945 − 241	976 − 405
765 − 102	
789 − 456	879 − 145
430 − 220	967 − 106
894 − 454	

Solve the problems.

If the difference is between	Color the shape
1 and 300	yellow
301 and 600	pink
601 and 1000	blue

Name _____

Iowa

STATE FACTS

Tree:
Oak

Flower:
Wild rose

Bird:
Eastern goldfinch

Capital:
Des Moines

STATE FLAG

IOWA

STATE CHALLENGE!

The lowest point in Iowa is 480 feet above sea level. The lowest point in Ohio is 455 feet above sea level. What is the difference in height between the two locations?

_____

The quilt contains the following problems:

934 − 782

614 − 252

834 − 464

967 − 277

509 − 459

837 − 169

357 − 349

476 − 238

758 − 373

664 − 476

289 − 197

886 − 192

835 − 586

992 − 267

787 − 197

516 − 464

522 − 149

Solve the problems.

If the difference is between	Color the shape
1 and 300	red
301 and 600	dark orange
601 and 1000	blue

Fill in the other shapes with colors of your choice.

Kansas

$$2 \times 11$$

$$2 \times 3$$

$$6 \times 2$$

$$5 \times 2$$

$$4 \times 2$$

$$10 \times 2$$

$$1 \times 2$$

$$2 \times 2$$

$$8 \times 2$$

$$2 \times 12$$

$$9 \times 2$$

$$2 \times 7$$

$$2 \times 6$$

$$11 \times 2$$

$$2 \times 10$$

$$2 \times 5$$

$$3 \times 2$$

$$2 \times 4$$

$$12 \times 2$$

$$2 \times 1$$

$$2 \times 8$$

$$7 \times 2$$

$$2 \times 2$$

$$2 \times 9$$

**Solve the problems. Then on each line below,
write the name of a color that you like.**

If the product is between	Color the shape
1 and 8	_____
9 and 16	_____
17 and 24	_____

Fill in the other shapes with colors of your choice.

Kentucky

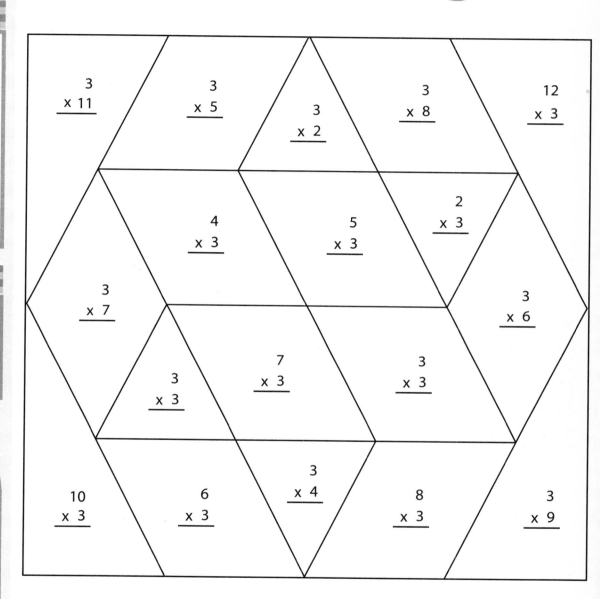

Solve the problems.

If the product is between	Color the shape
1 and 12	red
13 and 24	black
25 and 36	gray

Name _____

Louisiana

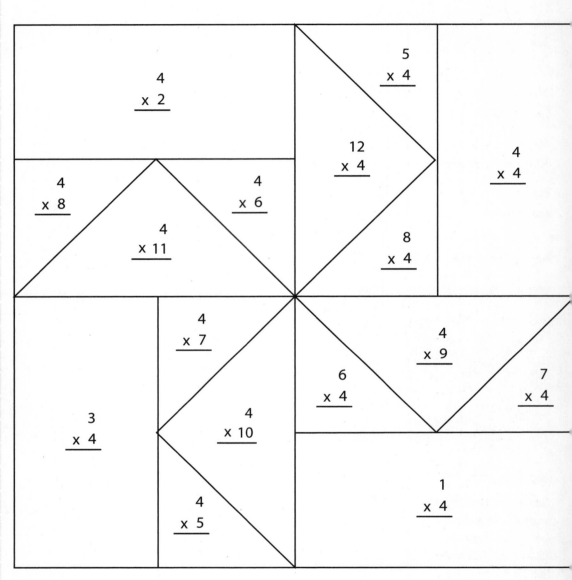

Within the quilt:

4 × 2

5 × 4

12 × 4

4 × 4

4 × 8

4 × 6

4 × 11

8 × 4

4 × 7

4 × 9

6 × 4

7 × 4

3 × 4

4 × 10

1 × 4

4 × 5

Solve the problems.

If the product is between	Color the shape
1 and 16	purple
17 and 32	green
33 and 48	pink

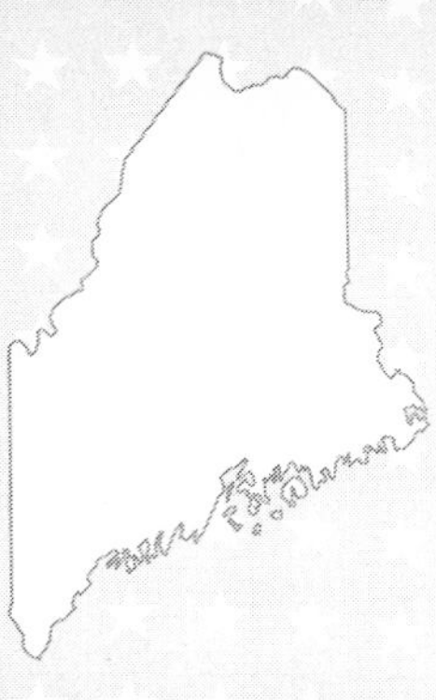

STATE FACTS

Tree:
White pine

Flower:
White pine cone and tassel

Bird:
Chickadee

Capital:
Augusta

STATE FLAG

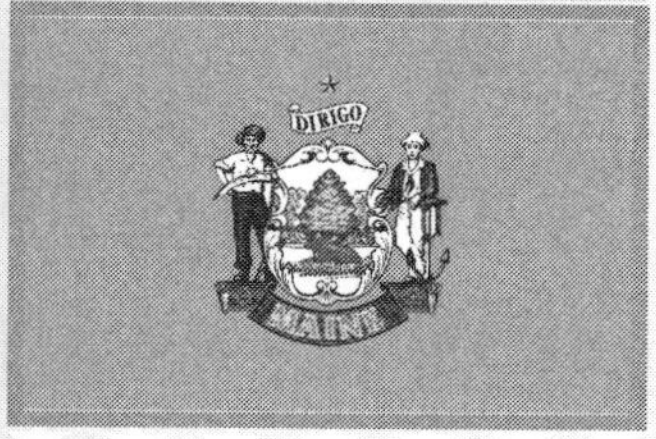

STATE CHALLENGE!

Maine's state animal is the moose. It is the largest member of the deer family. If there are two groups of five moose, how many animals are there in all?

____

Name ______________________________

Multiplication: 5's

Maine

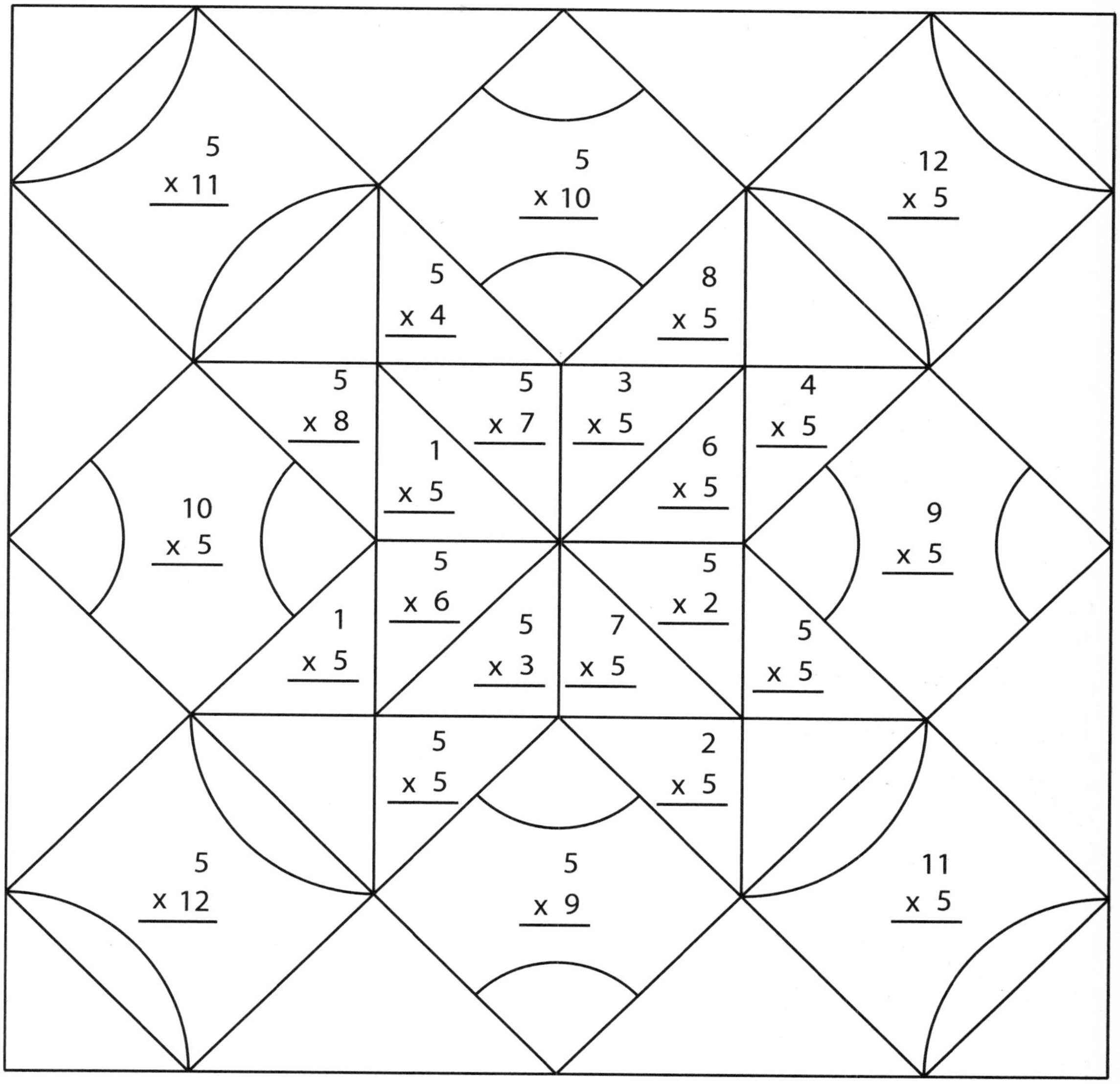

Solve the problems.

If the product is between	Color the shape
1 and 20	pink
21 and 40	purple
41 and 60	light blue

Fill in the other shapes with colors of your choice.

Maryland

STATE FACTS

Tree:
White oak

Flower:
Black-eyed Susan

Bird:
Baltimore oriole

Capital:
Annapolis

STATE FLAG

STATE CHALLENGE!

Maryland's state boat is the Skipjack. Ellen has a collection of Skipjack model boats and she is sending them to the statehouse for display. She sent two boxes with six boats in each box. What is the total number of model boats she sent?

_____

10 × 6	6 × 3

| 1 × 6 | 6 × 12 |

| 3 × 6 | 5 × 6 | 8 × 6 | 4 × 6 | 7 × 6 | 6 × 1 |

| 11 × 6 | 6 × 10 |

| 1 × 6 |

| 6 × 3 | 6 × 10 | 12 × 6 | 2 × 6 |

| 6 × 5 | 6 × 7 | 6 × 6 | 9 × 6 |

| 12 × 6 | 6 × 2 | 1 × 6 | 6 × 11 |

Solve the problems.

If the product is between	Color the shape
1 and 18	yellow
19 and 36	dark blue
37 and 54	orange
55 and 72	blue

Fill in the other shapes with colors of your choice.

Massachusetts

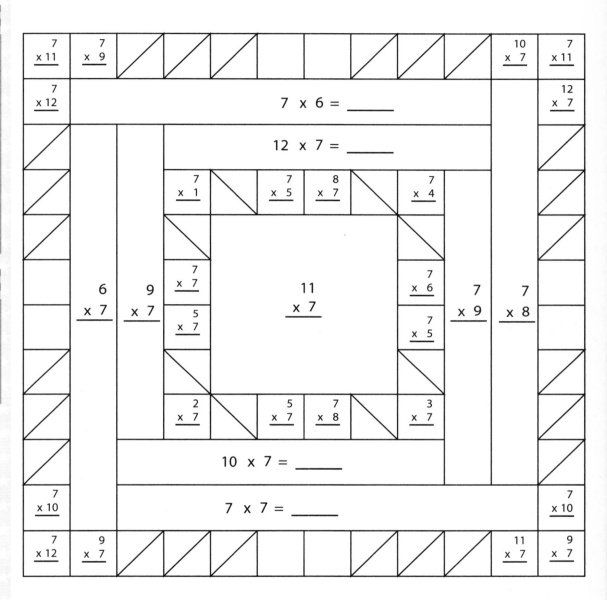

Solve the problems.

If the product is between	Color the shape
1 and 28	dark blue
29 and 56	yellow
57 and 84	green

Fill in the other shapes with colors of your choice.

Michigan

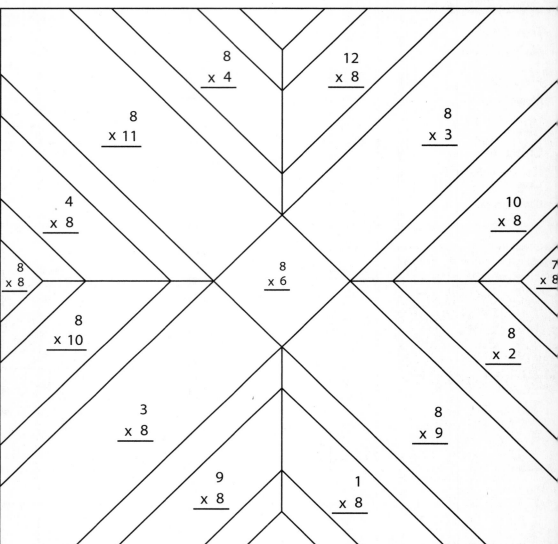

$$
\begin{array}{r} 8 \\ \times\ 4 \\ \hline \end{array}
\qquad
\begin{array}{r} 12 \\ \times\ 8 \\ \hline \end{array}
$$

$$
\begin{array}{r} 8 \\ \times\ 11 \\ \hline \end{array}
\qquad
\begin{array}{r} 8 \\ \times\ 3 \\ \hline \end{array}
$$

$$
\begin{array}{r} 4 \\ \times\ 8 \\ \hline \end{array}
\qquad
\begin{array}{r} 10 \\ \times\ 8 \\ \hline \end{array}
$$

$$
\begin{array}{r} 8 \\ \times\ 8 \\ \hline \end{array}
\qquad
\begin{array}{r} 8 \\ \times\ 6 \\ \hline \end{array}
\qquad
\begin{array}{r} 7 \\ \times\ 8 \\ \hline \end{array}
$$

$$
\begin{array}{r} 8 \\ \times\ 10 \\ \hline \end{array}
\qquad
\begin{array}{r} 8 \\ \times\ 2 \\ \hline \end{array}
$$

$$
\begin{array}{r} 3 \\ \times\ 8 \\ \hline \end{array}
\qquad
\begin{array}{r} 8 \\ \times\ 9 \\ \hline \end{array}
$$

$$
\begin{array}{r} 9 \\ \times\ 8 \\ \hline \end{array}
\qquad
\begin{array}{r} 1 \\ \times\ 8 \\ \hline \end{array}
$$

**Solve the problems. Then on each line below,
write the name of a color that you like.**

If the product is between	Color the shape
1 and 32	_____
33 and 64	_____
65 and 96	_____

Fill in the other shapes with colors of your choice.

Minnesota

The quilt puzzle contains the following multiplication problems:

- 4 x 9
- 1 x 9
- 9 x 12
- 10 x 9
- 1 x 9
- 9 x 9
- 12 x 9
- 6 x 9
- 2 x 9
- 9 x 2
- 3 x 9
- 9 x 3
- 9 x 6
- 11 x 9
- 9 x 10
- 9 x 3
- 9 x 11
- 9 x 9
- 9 x 2
- 9 x 5

Solve the problems.

If the product is between	Color the shape
1 and 28	light blue
29 and 56	pink
57 and 106	light green

Fill in the other shapes with colors of your choice.

Name _____

Mississippi

STATE FACTS

Tree:
Magnolia

Flower:
Magnolia

Bird:
Mockingbird

Capital:
Jackson

STATE FLAG

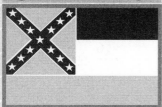

STATE CHALLENGE!

Yazoo city is 51 miles from the city of Vicksburg in Mississippi. The city of Greenwood is twice as far away. How far is Greenwood from Vicksburg?

_____

```
        32
        x 6
47          56          84
x 9         x 5         x 8
      22
      x 6

79                      68
x 2                     x 2
68          86          65
x 5         x 7         x 6
      52                      29
      x 3                     x 4

                  41
                  x 4
95          34          56
x 7         x 9         x 9
      19
      x 5
```

**Solve the problems. Then on each line below,
write the name of a color that you like.**

If the product is between	Color the shape
1 and 200	_____
201 and 400	_____
401 and 900	_____

Missouri

STATE FACTS

Tree:
Flowering dogwood

Flower:
Hawthorn

Bird:
Bluebird

Capital:
Jefferson City

STATE FLAG

STATE CHALLENGE!

In the year 2000, Matthews City, Missouri had a population of 606 people. The city of Maysville had a population twice as large. How many people lived in Maysville in that year?

299
x 9

677
x 2

780
x 8

199
x 5

530
x 4

652
x 4

978
x 7

219
x 2

890
x 8

518
x 3

718
x 5

602
x 4

525
x 2

789
x 8

918
x 9

617
x 3

699
x 9

676
x 7

901
x 3

867
x 5

Solve the problems.

If the product is between	Color the shape
1 and 2000	orange
2001 and 6000	yellow
6001 and 9000	blue

Name _____

Montana

```
55        80
x 87      x 73

76        55        87
x 97      x 12      x 86

          98   83   70
          x 33 x 60 x 42

29   81   57   79        56
x 32 x 72 x 33 x 63      x 30

     71   85   53
     x 38 x 66 x 51

79        37        99
x 86      x 29      x 78

59                       62
x 78                     x 80
```

Solve the problems.

If the product is between	Color the shape
1 and 2000	red
2001 and 4000	purple
4001 and 6000	yellow
6001 and 10,000	blue

Fill in the other shapes with colors of your choice.

nebraska

STATE FACTS

Tree:
Cottonwood

Flower:
Goldenrod

Bird:
Western
meadowlark

Capital:
Lincoln

STATE FLAG

STATE CHALLENGE!

Nebraska is about
430 miles long. Hiro
figured out that if his
family drove a straight
path going 40 miles
an hour, it would take
a little over 11 hours
to cross the state. Is he
correct? Explain your
answer on the back of
this page.

199 x 21	682 x 63	421 x 20	738 x 97	299 x 16	834 x 33	108 x 13
587 x 71						983 x 41
101 x 13		312 x 24				215 x 20
698 x 84	375 x 19	501 x 65	401 x 21			904 x 87
255 x 27		423 x 20				220 x 31
650 x 70						687 x 67
311 x 12	923 x 43	209 x 17	789 x 82	140 x 15	576 x 81	155 x 25

Solve the problems.

If the product is between	Color the shape
1 and 10,000	red
10,001 and 50,000	blue
51,001 and 99,000	yellow

Fill in the other shapes with colors of your choice.

nevada

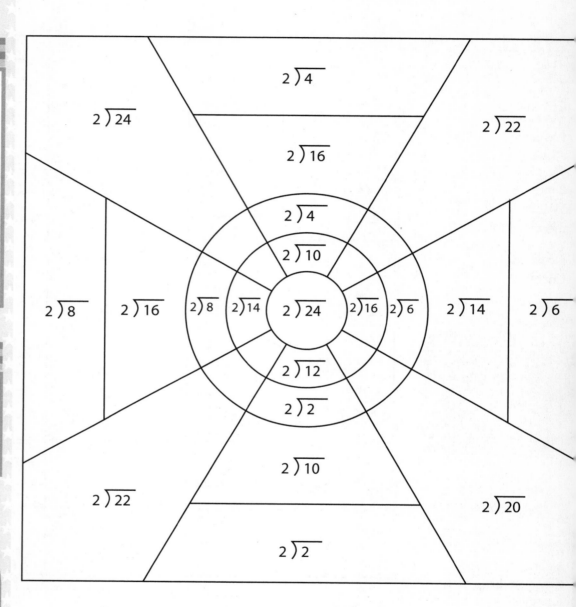

Solve the problems.

If the quotient is between	Color the shape
1 and 4	blue
5 and 9	dark orange
10 and 12	purple

Fill in the other shapes with colors of your choice.

new Hampshire

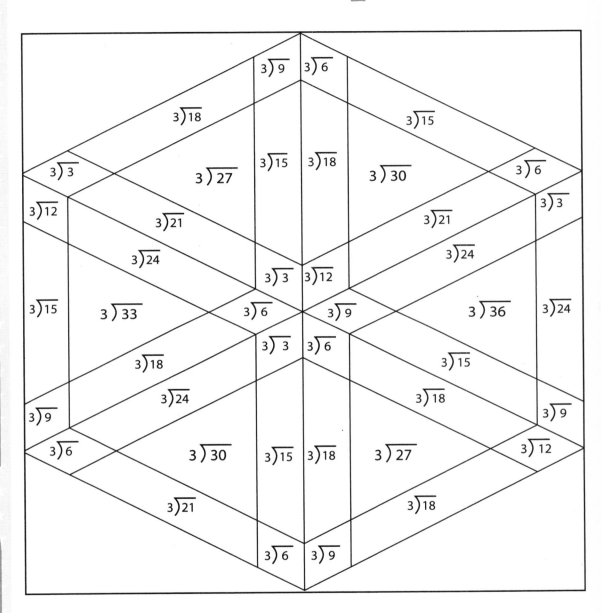

Solve the problems.

If the quotient is between	Color the shape
1 and 4	blue
5 and 8	green
9 and 12	yellow

Fill in the other shapes with colors of your choice.

Name _____

new Jersey

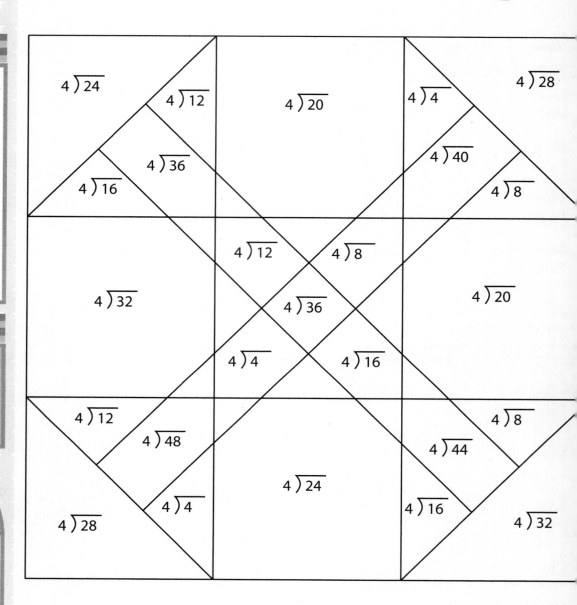

Solve the problems.

If the quotient is between	Color the shape
1 and 4	dark blue
5 and 8	yellow
9 and 12	pink

Fill in the other shapes with colors of your choice.

new Mexico

STATE FACTS

Tree:
Piñon

Flower:
Yucca flower

Bird:
Roadrunner

Capital:
Santa Fe

STATE FLAG

STATE CHALLENGE!

New Mexico's state gem is the turquoise. Alicia is making 5 identical bracelets. If she has 45 turquoise beads, how many should she use for each bracelet?

_____

$5\overline{)45}$ $5\overline{)55}$ $5\overline{)25}$ $5\overline{)45}$ $5\overline{)50}$

$5\overline{)35}$ $5\overline{)10}$ $5\overline{)5}$ $5\overline{)40}$

$5\overline{)5}$ $5\overline{)5}$ $5\overline{)10}$

$5\overline{)55}$ $5\overline{)30}$ $5\overline{)55}$

$5\overline{)10}$

$5\overline{)40}$ $5\overline{)50}$ $5\overline{)35}$

$5\overline{)60}$ $5\overline{)15}$ $5\overline{)60}$

$5\overline{)15}$ $5\overline{)25}$ $5\overline{)20}$

$5\overline{)20}$

$5\overline{)40}$ $5\overline{)20}$ $5\overline{)15}$ $5\overline{)30}$

$5\overline{)30}$

$5\overline{)55}$ $5\overline{)60}$ $5\overline{)50}$ $5\overline{)45}$

Solve the problems.

If the quotient is between	Color the shape
1 and 4	orange
5 and 8	brown
9 and 12	black

Fill in the other shapes with colors of your choice.

Name _____

new york

STATE FACTS

Tree:
Sugar maple

Flower:
Rose

Bird:
Bluebird

Capital:
Albany

STATE FLAG

STATE CHALLENGE!

New York's state fruit is the apple. Nolan picked 54 apples and said that he put the same number of apples in 6 bags. One of the bags has 8 apples in it. Do you think Nolan divided them evenly? Explain your answer on the back of this page.

$6\overline{)42}$ $6\overline{)54}$ $6\overline{)48}$ $6\overline{)72}$

$6\overline{)6}$ $6\overline{)12}$

$6\overline{)18}$ $6\overline{)6}$

$6\overline{)42}$ $6\overline{)36}$ $6\overline{)42}$ $6\overline{)24}$

$6\overline{)12}$ $6\overline{)18}$

$6\overline{)54}$ $6\overline{)18}$ $6\overline{)12}$ $6\overline{)54}$ $6\overline{)66}$

$6\overline{)48}$

$6\overline{)30}$

$6\overline{)60}$

$6\overline{)36}$

Solve the problems.

If the quotient is between	Color the shape
1 and 3	red
4 and 6	black
7 and 9	yellow
10 and 12	blue

north Carolina

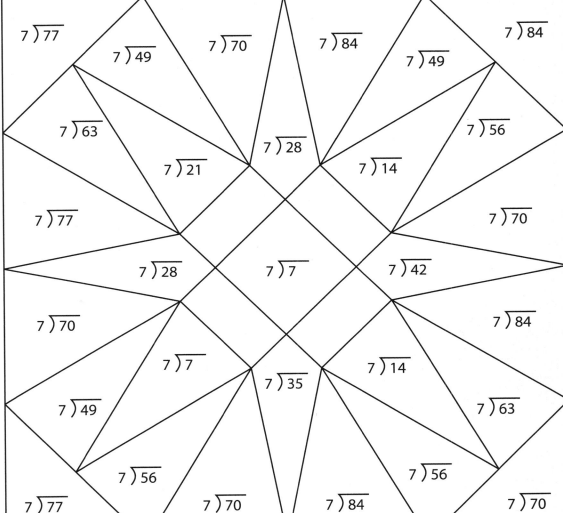

$7\overline{)77}$ $7\overline{)49}$ $7\overline{)70}$ $7\overline{)84}$ $7\overline{)84}$
$7\overline{)49}$ $7\overline{)63}$ $7\overline{)28}$ $7\overline{)56}$
$7\overline{)21}$ $7\overline{)14}$
$7\overline{)77}$ $7\overline{)70}$
$7\overline{)28}$ $7\overline{)7}$ $7\overline{)42}$
$7\overline{)70}$ $7\overline{)84}$
$7\overline{)7}$ $7\overline{)14}$
$7\overline{)49}$ $7\overline{)35}$ $7\overline{)63}$
$7\overline{)56}$ $7\overline{)56}$
$7\overline{)77}$ $7\overline{)70}$ $7\overline{)84}$ $7\overline{)70}$

STATE CHALLENGE!

North Carolina's state vegetable is the sweet potato. Daryl has 55 sweet potatoes and would like to divide them evenly among 7 people. Is this possible? Explain your answer on the back of this page.

Solve the problems.

If the quotient is between	Color the shape
1 and 3	red
4 and 6	green
7 and 9	yellow
10 and 12	light blue

Fill in the other shapes with colors of your choice.

north Dakota

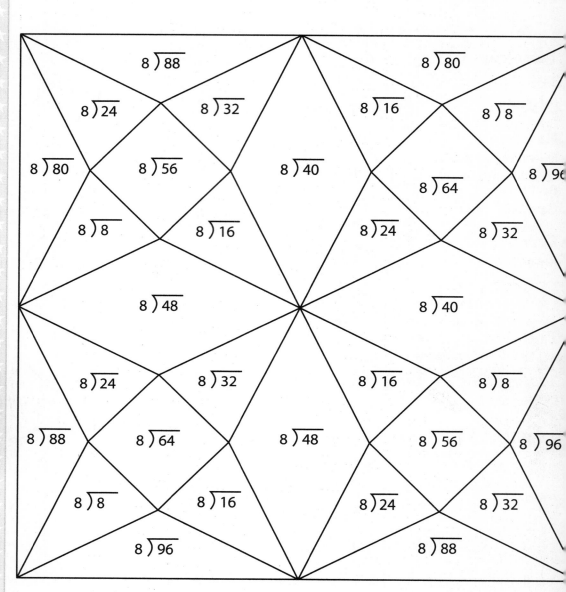

Solve the problems.

If the quotient is between	Color the shape
1 and 4	red
5 and 6	green
7 and 9	yellow
10 and 12	purple

Ohio

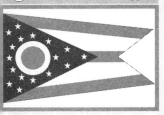
$9\overline{)9}$

$9\overline{)90}$ $9\overline{)72}$ $9\overline{)54}$ $9\overline{)99}$

$9\overline{)18}$

$9\overline{)27}$ $9\overline{)27}$

$9\overline{)54}$ $9\overline{)63}$ $9\overline{)99}$ $9\overline{)72}$ $9\overline{)45}$

$9\overline{)18}$ $9\overline{)36}$

$9\overline{)9}$

$9\overline{)81}$ $9\overline{)63}$ $9\overline{)45}$ $9\overline{)108}$

$9\overline{)36}$

Solve the problems.

If the quotient is between	Color the shape
1 and 4	red
5 and 8	black
9 and 12	green

Name _____

Oklahoma

STATE CHALLENGE!

The Yung family is driving 130 miles from Oklahoma City to the city of McAlester. They want to stop and eat at the halfway point. How many miles will they travel before stopping to eat?

_____

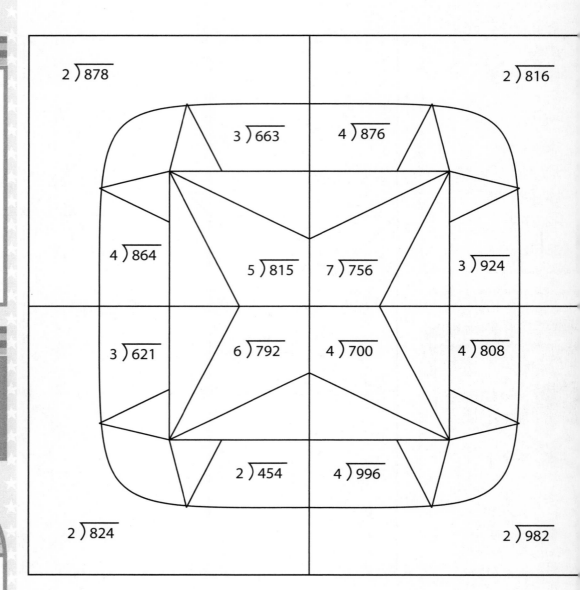

$2\overline{)878}$

$2\overline{)816}$

$3\overline{)663}$ $4\overline{)876}$

$4\overline{)864}$

$5\overline{)815}$ $7\overline{)756}$

$3\overline{)924}$

$3\overline{)621}$ $6\overline{)792}$ $4\overline{)700}$ $4\overline{)808}$

$2\overline{)454}$ $4\overline{)996}$

$2\overline{)824}$

$2\overline{)982}$

Solve the problems.

If the quotient is between	Color the shape
1 and 200	yellow
201 and 400	purple
401 and 1000	black

Fill in the other shapes with colors of your choice.

Name _____

Oregon

STATE FACTS

Tree:
Douglas fir

Flower:
Oregon grape

Bird:
Western
meadowlark

Capital:
Salem

STATE FLAG

STATE OF OREGON

1859

STATE CHALLENGE!

The coastline of Oregon is about 296 miles long. Adam calculated that if he walked 9 miles a day, he could walk the entire coastline in less than 31 days. Do you agree with Adam? Explain your answer on the back of this page.

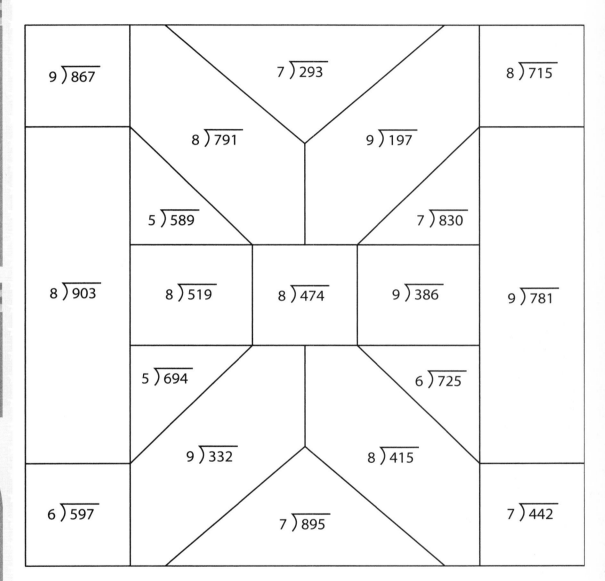

$9 \overline{)867}$ $7 \overline{)293}$ $8 \overline{)715}$

$8 \overline{)791}$ $9 \overline{)197}$

$5 \overline{)589}$ $7 \overline{)830}$

$8 \overline{)903}$ $8 \overline{)519}$ $8 \overline{)474}$ $9 \overline{)386}$ $9 \overline{)781}$

$5 \overline{)694}$ $6 \overline{)725}$

$9 \overline{)332}$ $8 \overline{)415}$

$6 \overline{)597}$ $7 \overline{)895}$ $7 \overline{)442}$

Solve the problems.

If the remainder is between	Color the shape
1 and 3	orange
4 and 6	green
7 and 9	blue

Name _____

Pennsylvania

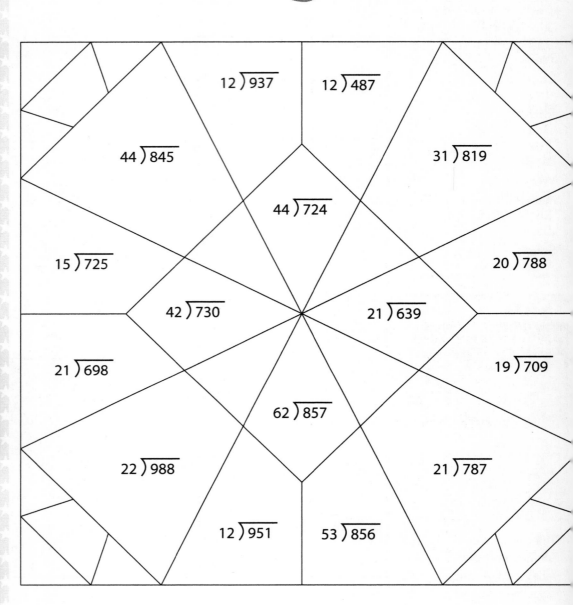

$12 \overline{)937}$ $12 \overline{)487}$

$44 \overline{)845}$ $31 \overline{)819}$

$44 \overline{)724}$

$15 \overline{)725}$ $20 \overline{)788}$

$42 \overline{)730}$ $21 \overline{)639}$

$21 \overline{)698}$ $19 \overline{)709}$

$62 \overline{)857}$

$22 \overline{)988}$ $21 \overline{)787}$

$12 \overline{)951}$ $53 \overline{)856}$

Solve the problems.

If the remainder is between	Color the shape
0 and 8	purple
9 and 60	red

Fill in the other shapes with colors of your choice.

Rhode Island

STATE FACTS

Tree:
Red maple

Flower:
Violet

Bird:
Rhode Island red

Capital:
Providence

STATE FLAG

STATE CHALLENGE!

In July 2005, Rhode Island had 2.07 inches of rain. In August of that year, the state had 4.18 inches of rain. How many inches of rain fell in all during these two months?

_____

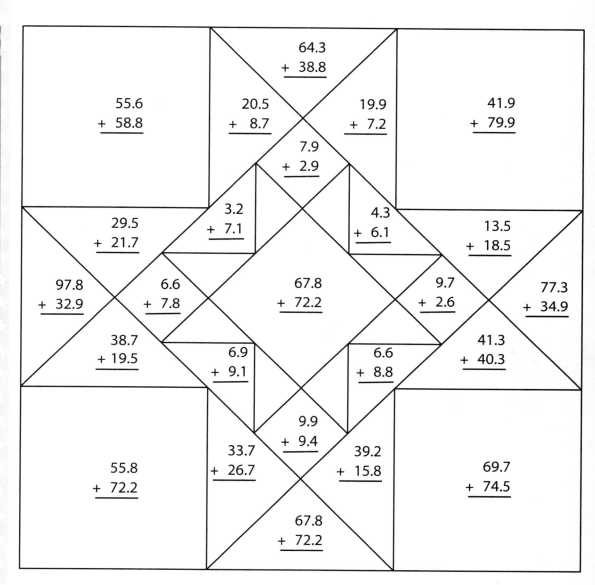

Quilt problems:

64.3 + 38.8

55.6 + 58.8

20.5 + 8.7

19.9 + 7.2

41.9 + 79.9

7.9 + 2.9

29.5 + 21.7

3.2 + 7.1

4.3 + 6.1

13.5 + 18.5

97.8 + 32.9

6.6 + 7.8

67.8 + 72.2

9.7 + 2.6

77.3 + 34.9

38.7 + 19.5

6.9 + 9.1

6.6 + 8.8

41.3 + 40.3

9.9 + 9.4

33.7 + 26.7

39.2 + 15.8

69.7 + 74.5

55.8 + 72.2

67.8 + 72.2

**Solve the problems. Then on each line below,
write the name of a color that you like.**

If the sum is between	Color the shape
1 and 20	_____
21 and 100	_____
101 and 200	_____

Fill in the other shapes with colors of your choice.

South Carolina

STATE FACTS

Tree:
Palmetto

Flower:
Yellow jessamine

Bird:
Carolina wren

Capital:
Columbia

STATE FLAG

STATE CHALLENGE!

South Carolina's highest average monthly temperature is 91.9°F. Its lowest average monthly temperature is 60.7 degrees less. What is the lowest average monthly temperature there?

_____

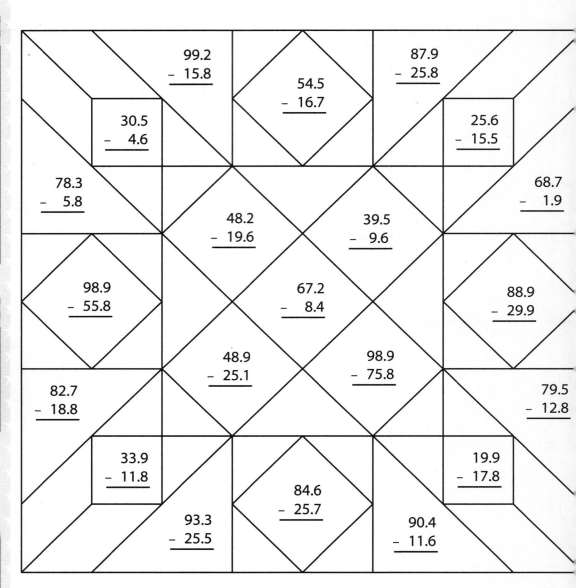

Solve the problems.

If the difference is between	Color the shape
1 and 30	pink
31 and 60	green
61 and greater	red

Fill in the other shapes with colors of your choice.

Name _____

South Dakota

STATE FACTS

Tree:
Black Hills spruce

Flower:
Pasqueflower

Bird:
Ring-necked pheasant

Capital:
Pierre

STATE FLAG

STATE CHALLENGE!

Fry bread is the official state bread of South Dakota. Elizabeth is making four batches of fry bread. If she needs 2.5 pounds of flour for each batch, how many pounds of flour will she need in all?

_____

Quilt problems:

- 68.4 × 7
- 42.7 × 5
- 79.3 × 6
- 93.4 × 6
- 82.8 × 9
- 60.1 × 2
- 90.1 × 5
- 22.8 × 7
- 56.3 × 3
- 66.1 × 8
- 6.8 × 7
- 9.3 × 6
- 2.1 × 2
- 8.6 × 3
- 58.9 × 8
- 46.8 × 3
- 92.5 × 3
- 90.1 × 9
- 92.1 × 2
- 49.5 × 9
- 76.7 × 6
- 74.2 × 6
- 89.4 × 4
- 88.1 × 7

Solve the problems.

If the product is between	Color the shape
1 and 100	purple
101 and 400	pink
401 and 900	yellow

Fill in the other shapes with colors of your choice.

Tennessee

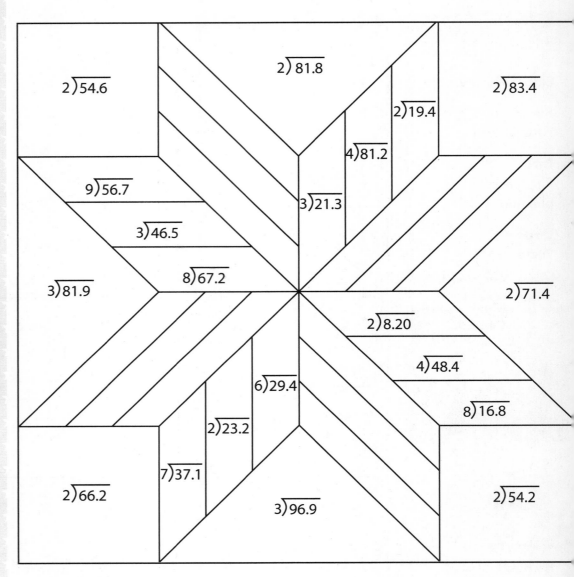

Solve the problems.

If the quotient is between	Color the shape
1 and 10	blue
11 and 25	yellow
26 and 49	red

Fill in the other shapes with colors of your choice.

Name _____

Texas

STATE FACTS

Tree:
Pecan

Flower:
Bluebonnet

Bird:
Mockingbird

Capital:
Austin

STATE FLAG

STATE CHALLENGE!

The Texas state dish is chili. Alexi made 6 quarts of chili and served it at a party. He had $\frac{1}{3}$ of the chili leftover. How many quarts did he have left?

_____

$\frac{4}{7} = \frac{28}{}$

$\frac{3}{5} = \frac{15}{}$

$\frac{8}{9} = \frac{16}{}$

$\frac{5}{12} = \frac{}{24}$

$\frac{6}{7} = \frac{}{14}$

$\frac{2}{3} = \frac{}{9}$

$\frac{1}{2} = \frac{}{10}$

$\frac{2}{7} = \frac{}{21}$

$\frac{1}{7} = \frac{2}{}$

$\frac{1}{2} = \frac{8}{}$

$\frac{1}{4} = \frac{2}{}$

$\frac{1}{5} = \frac{}{15}$

$\frac{3}{5} = \frac{}{25}$

$\frac{2}{10} = \frac{10}{}$

$\frac{10}{13} = \frac{}{39}$

Find the equivalent fractions.

If the answer is between	Color the shape
0 and 10	yellow
11 and 22	blue
23 and 90	green

utah

STATE FACTS

Tree:
Blue spruce

Flower:
Sego lily

Bird:
California gull

Capital:
Salt Lake City

STATE FLAG

STATE CHALLENGE!

The historic state vegetable of Utah is the sugar beet. Nita has $\frac{6}{12}$ of a cup of diced sugar beets. The recipe she is using calls for $\frac{1}{2}$ cup of diced sugar beets. Does she have enough? Explain your answer on the back of this page.

_____

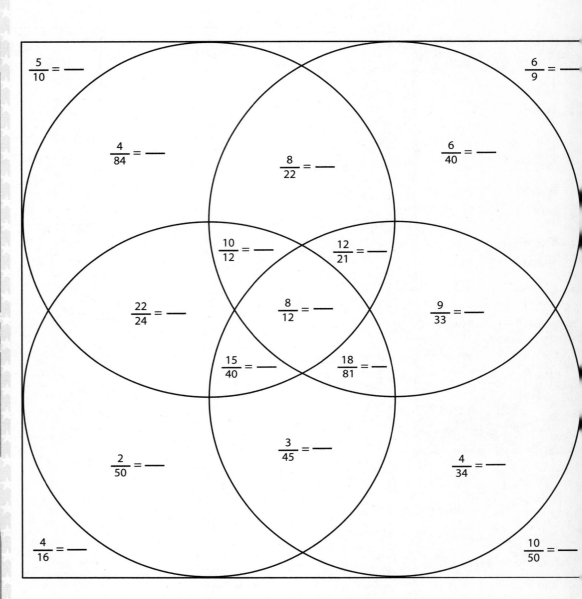

$\frac{5}{10} = \underline{\quad}$ $\frac{6}{9} = \underline{\quad}$

$\frac{4}{84} = \underline{\quad}$ $\frac{8}{22} = \underline{\quad}$ $\frac{6}{40} = \underline{\quad}$

$\frac{10}{12} = \underline{\quad}$ $\frac{12}{21} = \underline{\quad}$

$\frac{22}{24} = \underline{\quad}$ $\frac{8}{12} = \underline{\quad}$ $\frac{9}{33} = \underline{\quad}$

$\frac{15}{40} = \underline{\quad}$ $\frac{18}{81} = \underline{\quad}$

$\frac{2}{50} = \underline{\quad}$ $\frac{3}{45} = \underline{\quad}$ $\frac{4}{34} = \underline{\quad}$

$\frac{4}{16} = \underline{\quad}$ $\frac{10}{50} = \underline{\quad}$

Rename each fraction in lowest terms.

If the denominator in the answer is between	Color the shape
0 and 5	yellow
6 and 10	orange
11 and 15	blue
16 and 100	purple

Vermont

The quilt contains the following problems:

$$\frac{4}{13} + \frac{4}{13} = \underline{\quad}$$

$$\frac{6}{21} + \frac{1}{21}$$

$$\frac{4}{18} + \frac{5}{18}$$

$$\frac{5}{25} + \frac{5}{25}$$

$$\frac{9}{17} + \frac{1}{17}$$

$$\frac{4}{15} + \frac{4}{15}$$

$$\frac{4}{10} + \frac{4}{10}$$

$$\frac{5}{14} + \frac{2}{14}$$

$$\frac{2}{10} + \frac{1}{10}$$

$$\frac{3}{16} + \frac{5}{16}$$

$$\frac{2}{9} + \frac{5}{9} = \underline{\quad}$$

$$\frac{2}{7} + \frac{4}{7} = \underline{\quad}$$

$$\frac{1}{19} + \frac{5}{19}$$

$$\frac{8}{40} + \frac{2}{40}$$

$$\frac{8}{30} + \frac{7}{30}$$

$$\frac{7}{12} + \frac{2}{12}$$

$$\frac{9}{11} + \frac{1}{11}$$

$$\frac{9}{25} + \frac{10}{25}$$

$$\frac{3}{20} + \frac{1}{20}$$

$$\frac{2}{12} + \frac{1}{12}$$

$$\frac{4}{16} + \frac{4}{16}$$

$$\frac{2}{8} + \frac{4}{8} = \underline{\quad}$$

Solve the problems. Rename in lowest terms.

If the sum is	Color the shape
$\frac{1}{2}$ or less	green
greater than $\frac{1}{2}$	yellow

Fill in the other shapes with colors of your choice.

Name _____

Virginia

STATE FACTS

Tree:
Flowering dogwood

Flower:
Flowering dogwood

Bird:
Cardinal

Capital:
Richmond

STATE FLAG

STATE CHALLENGE!

The Virginia state beverage is milk. Peter will serve milk to his classmates when he gives a presentation on Virginia. If he takes $\frac{1}{2}$ gallon of whole milk and $\frac{1}{4}$ gallon of skim milk, how much milk will he have in all?

_____

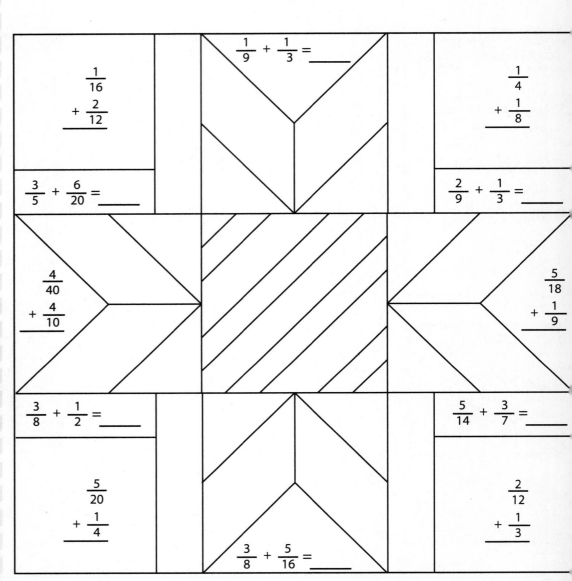

$\frac{1}{9} + \frac{1}{3} =$ _____

$\frac{1}{16} + \frac{2}{12}$ _____

$\frac{1}{4} + \frac{1}{8}$ _____

$\frac{3}{5} + \frac{6}{20} =$ _____

$\frac{2}{9} + \frac{1}{3} =$ _____

$\frac{4}{40} + \frac{4}{10}$ _____

$\frac{5}{18} + \frac{1}{9}$ _____

$\frac{3}{8} + \frac{1}{2} =$ _____

$\frac{5}{14} + \frac{3}{7} =$ _____

$\frac{5}{20} + \frac{1}{4}$ _____

$\frac{2}{12} + \frac{1}{3}$ _____

$\frac{3}{8} + \frac{5}{16} =$ _____

Solve the problems. Rename in lowest terms.

If the sum is	Color the shape
$\frac{1}{2}$ or less	red
greater than $\frac{1}{2}$	blue

Fill in the other shapes with colors of your choice.

Washington

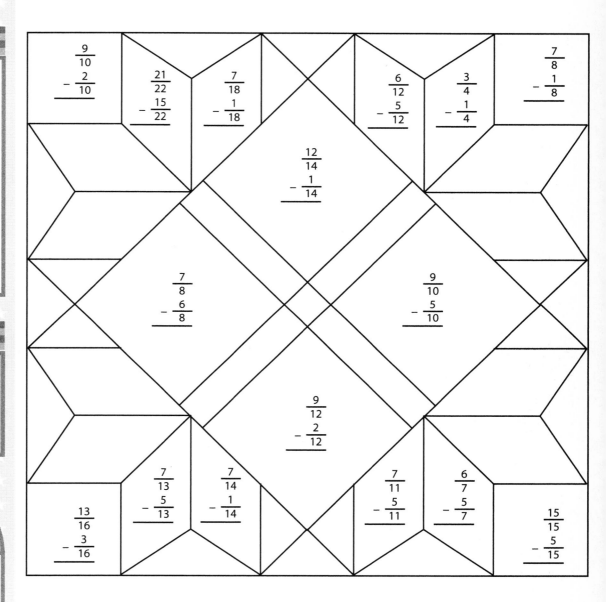

Solve each problem. Rename in lowest terms.

If the difference is	Color the shape
$\frac{1}{2}$ or less	pink
greater than $\frac{1}{2}$	dark red

Fill in the other shapes with colors of your choice.

West Virginia

STATE FACTS

Tree:
Sugar maple

Flower:
Rhododendron

Bird:
Cardinal

Capital:
Charleston

STATE FLAG

STATE CHALLENGE!

West Virginia's state tree is the sugar maple, and it produces maple syrup. Mrs. Jacob's class went to a farm and watched maple syrup being made. They brought seven-eighths of a gallon of syrup back to school. They gave three-fourths of a gallon to another class. How much did they have left?

_____

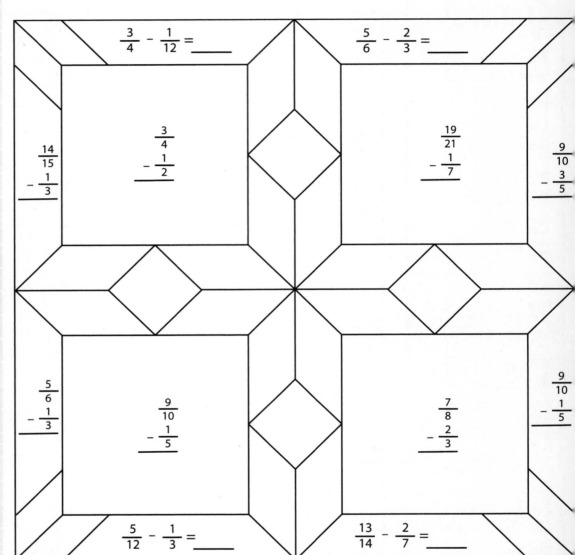

$\frac{3}{4} - \frac{1}{12} =$ _____

$\frac{5}{6} - \frac{2}{3} =$ _____

$\begin{array}{r} \frac{14}{15} \\ - \frac{1}{3} \\ \hline \end{array}$

$\begin{array}{r} \frac{3}{4} \\ - \frac{1}{2} \\ \hline \end{array}$

$\begin{array}{r} \frac{19}{21} \\ - \frac{1}{7} \\ \hline \end{array}$

$\begin{array}{r} \frac{9}{10} \\ - \frac{3}{5} \\ \hline \end{array}$

$\begin{array}{r} \frac{5}{6} \\ - \frac{1}{3} \\ \hline \end{array}$

$\begin{array}{r} \frac{9}{10} \\ - \frac{1}{5} \\ \hline \end{array}$

$\begin{array}{r} \frac{7}{8} \\ - \frac{2}{3} \\ \hline \end{array}$

$\begin{array}{r} \frac{9}{10} \\ - \frac{1}{5} \\ \hline \end{array}$

$\frac{5}{12} - \frac{1}{3} =$ _____

$\frac{13}{14} - \frac{2}{7} =$ _____

Solve each problem. Rename in lowest terms.

If the difference is	Color the shape
$\frac{1}{2}$ or less	yellow
greater than $\frac{1}{2}$	purple

Fill in the other shapes with colors of your choice.

Wisconsin

STATE FACTS

Tree:
Sugar maple

Flower:
Wood violet

Bird:
Robin

Capital:
Madison

STATE FLAG

WISCONSIN

1848

STATE CHALLENGE!

Luisa and her aunt camped in Devil's Lake State Park, one of the most popular parks in Wisconsin. Their campsite was located seven-eighths of a mile from a trailhead. They walked two-thirds of the way from their campsite to the trailhead before Luisa's dad picked them up. How far did they walk?

_____

$\frac{2}{5}$
$x \ \frac{1}{2}$

$\frac{5}{6} \times \frac{4}{5} =$ _____

$\frac{3}{4} \times \frac{2}{3} =$ _____

$\frac{5}{6}$
$x \ \frac{1}{3}$

$\frac{7}{8} \times \frac{8}{9} =$ _____

$\frac{3}{8}$
$x \ \frac{1}{3}$

$\frac{1}{4}$
$x \ \frac{1}{2}$

$\frac{6}{7} \times \frac{4}{5} =$ _____

$\frac{6}{7}$
$x \ \frac{2}{3}$

$\frac{7}{8} \times \frac{8}{11} =$ _____

$\frac{5}{8}$
$x \ \frac{3}{4}$

$\frac{1}{5}$
$x \ \frac{5}{6}$

$\frac{4}{5} \times \frac{2}{3} =$ _____

$\frac{10}{12} \times \frac{5}{6} =$ _____

$\frac{9}{10} \times \frac{4}{5} =$ _____

$\frac{1}{7}$
$x \ \frac{4}{7}$

$\frac{5}{7}$
$x \ \frac{1}{2}$

Solve each problem. Rename in lowest terms.

If the product is	Color the shape
less than $\frac{1}{2}$	gray
$\frac{1}{2}$ or greater	dark red

Fill in the other shapes with colors of your choice.

Wyoming

STATE FACTS

Tree:
Plains cottonwood

Flower:
Indian paintbrush

Bird:
Meadowlark

Capital:
Cheyenne

STATE FLAG

STATE CHALLENGE!

The Black Thunder mine in Wyoming is the largest coal mine in the United States. A contractor picks up $\frac{3}{4}$ of a ton of coal from the mine. He delivers $\frac{1}{8}$ of a ton to each of his clients. How many deliveries can he make?

_____

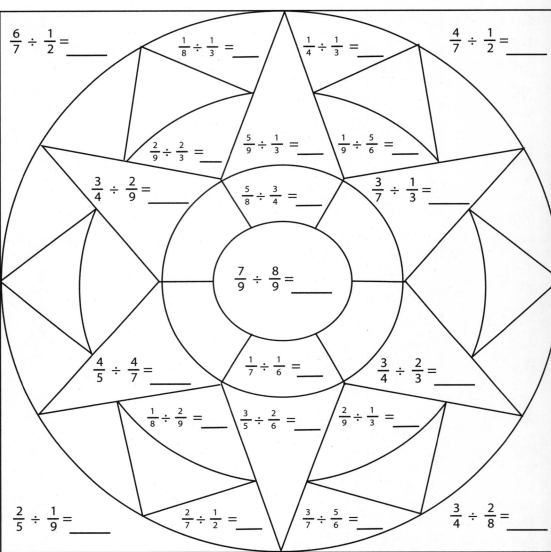

$\frac{6}{7} \div \frac{1}{2} =$ ____
$\frac{1}{8} \div \frac{1}{3} =$ ____
$\frac{1}{4} \div \frac{1}{3} =$ ____
$\frac{4}{7} \div \frac{1}{2} =$ ____

$\frac{2}{9} \div \frac{2}{3} =$ ____
$\frac{5}{9} \div \frac{1}{3} =$ ____
$\frac{1}{9} \div \frac{5}{6} =$ ____

$\frac{3}{4} \div \frac{2}{9} =$ ____
$\frac{5}{8} \div \frac{3}{4} =$ ____
$\frac{3}{7} \div \frac{1}{3} =$ ____

$\frac{7}{9} \div \frac{8}{9} =$ ____

$\frac{4}{5} \div \frac{4}{7} =$ ____
$\frac{1}{7} \div \frac{1}{6} =$ ____
$\frac{3}{4} \div \frac{2}{3} =$ ____

$\frac{1}{8} \div \frac{2}{9} =$ ____
$\frac{3}{5} \div \frac{2}{6} =$ ____
$\frac{2}{9} \div \frac{1}{3} =$ ____

$\frac{2}{5} \div \frac{1}{9} =$ ____
$\frac{2}{7} \div \frac{1}{2} =$ ____
$\frac{3}{7} \div \frac{5}{6} =$ ____
$\frac{3}{4} \div \frac{2}{8} =$ ____

Solve each problem. Rename in lowest terms.

If the quotient is	Color the shape
greater than 1	purple
less than or equal to 1	light blue

Fill in the other shapes with colors of your choice.

My Favorite Place

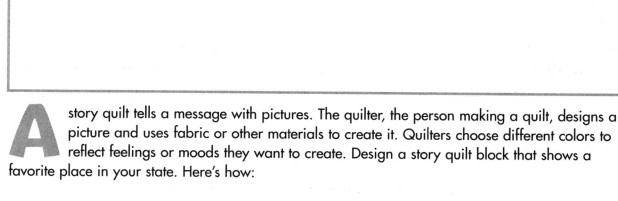

A story quilt tells a message with pictures. The quilter, the person making a quilt, designs a picture and uses fabric or other materials to create it. Quilters choose different colors to reflect feelings or moods they want to create. Design a story quilt block that shows a favorite place in your state. Here's how:

1. On a sheet of paper, draw a simple picture of a favorite place in your state.

2. Inside the quilt block outline above, recreate your picture using shapes cut from construction paper. For example, you might use a brown triangle to show a mountain or a blue oval for a lake. Add details using construction paper scraps.

3. Glue the construction paper shapes and pieces inside the quilt block.

On the back of this page, write a paragraph or two about your favorite place. Tell about when you discovered it and why it is special to you.

My Favorite Event

A story quilt tells a message with pictures. The quilter, the person making a quilt, designs a picture and uses fabric or other materials to create it. Quilters choose different colors to reflect feelings or moods they want to create. Design a story quilt block that shows a favorite event that takes place in your state. Here's how:

1. On a sheet of paper, draw a simple picture of a favorite event that takes place in your state.

2. Inside the quilt block outline above, recreate your picture using shapes cut from construction paper. Think about the colors that will work best. If the event is a happy one, you might use bright, cheerful colors. If it is patriotic, such as an Independence Day parade, you might choose red, white, and blue. Add details using construction paper scraps.

3. Glue the construction paper shapes and pieces inside the quilt block.

On the back of this page, write a paragraph or two about your favorite event. Tell about when you experienced it and why it is special to you.

My State's History

A story quilt tells a message with pictures. The quilter, the person making a quilt, designs a picture and uses fabric or other materials to create it. Quilters choose different colors to reflect feelings or moods they want to create. Design a story quilt block that shows an historic event that took place in your state. Here's how:

1. On a sheet of paper, draw a simple picture of an historic event that took place in your state.

2. Inside the quilt block outline on this page, recreate your picture using shapes cut from construction paper. Think about the colors that will work best. If the historic event is a sad one, you might use dark colors. If it is a celebration, you might use bold, eye-catching colors. Add details using construction paper scraps.

3. Glue the construction paper shapes and pieces inside the quilt block.

On the back of this page, write a paragraph or two about the historic event. Tell when, where, and why the event happened. What were the results?

Answers to the State Challenge Questions

Page 7:
tens: 2; ones: 2

Page 8:
3 is in the hundreds place

Page 9:
6,000

Page 10:
Arkansas had more than two million people.

Page 11:
California had fewer than one billion people.

Page 12:
7 is in the tenths place.

Page 13:
twenty-five and ninety-six hundredths

Page 14:
62 members

Page 15:
43 miles

Page 16:
296 people per square mile

Page 17:
$321

Page 18:
72 more people per square mile

Page 19:
9 states

Page 20:
about 140 miles wide

Page 21:
25 feet

Page 22:
12 eggs

Page 23:
12 freshwater pearls

Page 24:
32 agates

Page 25:
10 moose

Page 26:
12 boats

Page 27:
63 cookies

Page 28:
32 pictures

Page 29:
36 stickers

Page 30:
102 miles

Page 31:
1212 people

Page 32:
180 Montana agates

Page 33:
If Hiro's family drives for 11 hours at 40 mph, they would cover about 440 miles. Nebraska is 430

miles wide. So, Hiro is incorrect. It would take a little less than 11 hours to travel 430 miles.

Page 34:
9 pieces

Page 35:
Yes, if each friend got 9 ladybugs, they were divided evenly.

Page 36:
4 horses

Page 37:
9 beads

Page 38:
The apples were not divided evenly. Each bag should have 9 apples.

Page 39:
It is not possible to divide 55 sweet potatoes evenly among 7 people. If each person gets 7 sweet potatoes, there will be 6 leftover. There are not enough sweet potatoes to give each person 8.

Page 40:
Yes, you can divide 16 cartons of milk evenly among 8 people. Each person will get 2 cartons.

Page 41:
3 pieces

Page 42:
65 miles

Page 43:
If Adam were to walk 9 miles a day for 32 days, he would have walked 288 miles in all. Since the coastline of Oregon is about 296 miles long, it would take more than 31 days (32 R8), not less.

Page 44:
about 18 days (18 R4)

Page 45:
6.25 inches

Page 46:
31.2°F

Page 47:
10 pounds

Page 48:
12.9 inches

Page 49:
2 quarts leftover

Page 50:
She has enough sugar beets. $\frac{6}{12}$ and $\frac{1}{2}$ are equivalent fractions.

Page 51:
1 cup of sliced apples

Page 52:
$\frac{3}{4}$ gallon milk

Page 53:
$\frac{3}{8}$ bushel

Page 54:
$\frac{1}{8}$ quart

Page 55:
$\frac{7}{12}$ mile

page 56:
6 deliveries

Suggested Resources

U.S. States

Books

★ *The Look-It-Up Book of the 50 States* by Bill Gutman and Anne Wertheim (Random House, 2002). The beautiful illustrations in the book will captivate the most reluctant learner. The book contains a wide range of topics about each state including basic facts, climate and agricultural information, and fun places to visit.

★ *The Scholastic Atlas of the United States* by David Rubel (Scholastic, 2000). Organized by major geographical regions, this comprehensive resource includes clear, colorful maps and detailed information about major cities, highways, waterways, forests, mountain systems, national parks, reservations, and much more.

★ *The United States of America: A State-by-State Guide* by Millie Miller and Cyndi Nelson (Scholastic, 2001). This colorful guide provides information about each state ranging from state facts to biographical sketches of famous people. It is a perfect resource for students to use when compiling basic information about each state.

Web Sites

★ States and Capitals
www.50states.com
This Web site has extensive information about each state. It not only gives basic facts, such as the state flower, tree, bird, and capital, it also provides information on places to visit, famous people who lived there, and sports teams.

★ Fact Monster: The 50 States
www.factmonster.com/states
Here you'll find information on state history, natural resources, popular tourist locations, and more.

★ USDA: The Economics of Food, Farming, Natural Resources, and Rural America
www.ers.usda.gov/StateFacts
Produced by the United States Department of Agriculture, this site provides current data on the population, employment, income, education, and agriculture in each state.

If your students are interested in learning more about specific states, encourage them to use a search engine and search under the state's name. Many Web sites offer indepth information about specific states. (Always supervise students' use of the Internet.)

Quilts

Books

★ *Quilt-Block History of Pioneer Days* by Mary Cobb (The Millbrook Press, 1995). This delightful book tells the history of pioneer days through quilts. It includes pictures of dozens of quilt blocks and information about them, as well as projects that children can make.

★ *Quilt Math: Grades 4–6* by Cindi Mitchell (Scholastic, 2005). The 100 reproducible quilt math activities in this book provide even more opportunities for students to practice and master math skills. Topics include multi-digit addition and subtraction, multiplication and division, fractions, decimals, and more.

★ *Quick Quilts Across the Curriculum* by Kathy Pike, Jean Mumper, and Alice Fiske (Scholastic, 2003). Here you'll find dozens of cross-curricular project ideas with easy-to-follow directions on how to construct fun and appealing quilts, such as an Olympics plastic-bag quilt, a muffin-tin calendar quilt, an endangered species floor puzzle quilt, and much more.

★ *Quilt of States: Piecing Together America* by Adrienne Yorinks (National Geographic Society, 2005). The creator of this unique book has designed a quilt to represent each of the 50 states. Each design depicts things associated with a particular state. Two-page spreads include a photo of the quilt as well as information about the featured state, written by librarians from across the country.

★ *Traditional Quilts for Kids to Make* by Barbara J. Eilmeier (The Patchwork Place, 2001). This book includes eight traditional quilt plans and 15 traditional blocks designed especially for children to make. The author also teaches quiltmaking basics, from choosing fabric to hand-quilting.

★ *With Needle and Thread: A Book About Quilts* by Raymond Bial (Houghton Mifflin, 1996). The author explores the history of quilting in the United States including the economic and cultural factors that influence the designs, materials, and techniques used to make quilts.

★ *The United States Patchwork Pattern Book: 50 Quilt Blocks for 50 States from "Hearth & Home" Magazine*, selected and edited by Barbara Bannister and Edna P. Ford (Dover, 1976). Accompanying each of the 50 state quilt blocks in this collection are patterns and the yardage needed for making each quilt.

Web Sites

★ America's Quilting History
www.womenfolk.com/historyofquilts/
This site includes links to articles that explore the history of quiltmaking in the United States.

★ The History of Quilts in America
www.kathimitchell.com/quilt/quilt3.html
This site provides links to a variety of sources that offer information about the traditions of quilting.

★ International Quilt Study Center (IQSC) at the University of Nebraska-Lincoln
www.quiltstudy.org/exhibitions/current.html
The IQSC is dedicated to the collection, conservation, study, and exhibition of quilts. The site features numerous online exhibitions from the center's extensive collections.

★ The Quilt Index
www.quiltindex.org
This page on the Web site of the Alliance of American Quilts features collections of quilts from Kentucky, Illinois, Michigan, and Tennesse.

★ Quilts and Quiltmaking in America 1978-1996
http://memory.loc.gov/ammem/qlthtml/qlthome.html
The American Folklife Center on the Web site of the Library of Congress includes examples of quilts made by modern-day quilters from North Carolina and Virginia.

★ Quilts, Counterpanes & Throws
http://americanhistory.si.edu/collections/quilts/
Links to photographs of quilts that are part of the Smithsonian's extensive collection can be found here.

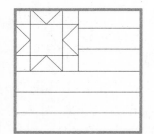 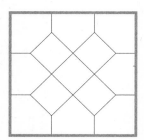 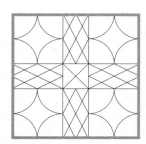 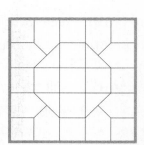